SURPRISE!
I HAVE A SECRET GIFT FOR MY DEAR READERS!

www.cj-caldwell.com/surprise

If you want to find out what it is, visit the URL and I'll send it to you directly.

(No e-mail address, registration or anything similar is required...)

C. J. CALDWELL

KETOGENIC COOKBOOK

OUTSTANDING KETOGENIC RECIPES
**THAT WILL SKYROCKET
YOUR FAT BURNING**
AND BOOST YOUR
KETO DIET
SUCCESS.

Disclaimer

The information provided within this book is for general informational purposes only. While we try to keep the information up-to-date and correct, there are no representations or warranties, express or implied, about the completeness, accuracy, reliability, suitability or availability with respect to the information, products, services, or related graphics contained in this eBook for any purpose. Any use of this information is at your own risk.

The methods describe within this book are the author's personal thoughts. They are not intended to be a definitive set of instructions for this project. You may discover there are other methods and materials to accomplish the same end result.

This book is not intended to be a substitute for the medical advice of a licensed physician. The reader should consult with their doctor in any matters relating to his/her health.

Copyright

Ketogenic Cookbook: Outstanding Ketogenic Recipes That Will Skyrocket Your Fat Burning and Boost Your Keto Diet Success
by Claudia J. Caldwell

Published by Florian Funk Publishing Consultant, Haus-Gravener Street 89, 40764 Langenfeld, Germany

www.cj-caldwell.com

© 2018 Claudia J. Caldwell | Florian Funk

All rights reserved. This book or parts thereof may not be reproduced in any form, stored in any retrieval system, or transmitted in any form by any means—electronic, mechanical, photocopy, recording, or otherwise—without prior written permission of the publisher, except as provided by United States of America copyright law. For permission requests, write to the publisher, at "Attention: Permissions Coordinator," at the address below.

Florian-Funk@gmx.net

ISBN: 9781980745556

Foreword

Dear Readers,

This cookbook is one of it's kind.

You won't find thousands of recipes in this book, like the cookbooks of big publishers. Also, you will not see any professionally shot footage of meals. I am an indie author, and I do not have the resources to create such a „perfect" book.

But, in this book, you'll find recipes that I've developed and improved over a long time. Recipes that I've poured my heart and soul into, Recipes that taste great.

And because words are sometimes not enough to express what you think and feel, I have recorded a personal voice message for you.

When you visit the URL below, my personal message is automatically sent to your messenger. Furthermore, I also have a little "secret" gift waiting for you.

Find out what I have to tell you:

www.cj-caldwell.com/secret

I will be grateful if you listen to my message.

I hope you enjoy reading this book, cooking the dishes and hopefully enjoying your new favorite recipes.

Best wishes,

Claudia J. Caldwell

TABLE OF CONTENTS

13	**Introduction**
17	**What is Ketogenic Diet**
26	**Benefits of Ketogenic Diet**
33	**Keto Diet Plan**
42	**Recipes**
43	**Breakfast**
44	• Poppy Seed Low Carb Bread
47	• Avocado Sunrise
49	• Brussels Sprout American Breakfast
51	• Keto Baba Ghanoush with Flatbread
56	• Scallion Halloumi American Breakfast
58	• Raspberry Pecan Pancake
60	• Coriander Shakshouka
63	**Lunch**
64	• Steamed Chicken Breast with Vegetables
67	• Keto Chicken Salad
70	• Spicy Cauliflower and Lamb
72	• Cauliflower and Chicken Thigh Bowl
75	• Spicy Cheeseburgers with Eggplants
78	• Grilled Flank Steak with Avocado Dip
81	• Stuffed Mushrooms and Zucchini
86	**Dinner**
87	• King Tabbouleh Salad

90   • Chicken and Spinach Supper
92   • Coconut Shrimp Soup
94   • Pork Loin with Broccoli
97   • Turkey Bacon and Chicken Meatballs
99   • Spicy Mushroom Soup
102 • Coconut Skirt Steak with Swiss Chard
105 **Feedback**
106 **Images and Layout**

Chapter 1

INTRODUCTION

After months of hearing about "Ketogenic diets" and its wonders, you finally decided to check it out. I'm glad you took this decision. In recent years, the Ketogenic diet, usually referred to as "keto", has been gaining momentum and all over the world; no doubt, there is a good reason for that.

In case you are wondering if keto is one of those modern-day fad diets, the answer is no. The keto diet did not start today. According to the history, this diet became popular in the 1920's when it was used as a treatment for diabetes and epilepsy. At the time, keto was developed to provide an alternative to non-mainstream fasting, which has proven to be successful as an epilepsy therapy.

Unfortunately, a couple of years later, new anticonvulsant therapies were developed for epilepsy, and keto was largely abandoned. Moreover, at the time, people weren't much concerned about their weight as they are today. This was perhaps, the reason you haven't heard about keto until recent years.
Apart from its numerous benefits, which we will discuss later in this book, the internet is one reason keto made a sudden resurgence in recent years.

Nowadays, it is easy for someone to share the success of their diet. You probably heard about the keto diet on the internet or from your gym instructor.

When it comes to weight loss, there are different opinions, hundreds of techniques, and thousands of diets. It seems like new diets are coming out daily. Most of these diets have made us believe the only way we can lose weight is through:

- Calorie restriction
- Intense exercise techniques
- Avoiding dietary fats

However, these have not kept down the rate at which the problem of obesity and overweight is increasing in most developed nations. Obesity and overweight lead to other issues, such as diabetes, increased heart risk, and more. In fact, according to research, an obese individual is likely to suffer from 50 more health problems than someone who isn't overweight. In recent years, there are a lot of researchers working anxiously on how to suppress appetite and achieve weight loss in a healthy, sustainable manner without harming the body. The keto diet is, perhaps, a testament to their effort.

Today, there are thousands of weight-loss diets on the internet with many claims of success. Most of these diets don't last more than a year because they were created by greedy marketers who want to tap into a multi-billion-dollar weight loss industry. Fortunately, the Keto diet is different from these fad diets that exist today. This diet is not only backed up by years of research and proven results. It's also been practiced for more than 90 years. The Keto diet is based upon a good understanding of nutrition science, as well as the physiology of the human body.

Over the years, many people have achieved varying degrees of positive results with ketogenic diets. The reason this diet works for so many people is that it targets several underlying causes of weight gain. Some of the key causes of weight gain that keto targets in the body include:

- Hormonal imbalances (e.g., insulin resistance)
- High blood sugar level

The principle behind this diet is different from other diets. It does not bother with relying on counting calories, limiting portion sizes, or making use of extreme exercise techniques to force weight loss. Moreover, the keto diet is easily practiced in your home without subscribing to any expensive package meal plan.

Keto helps you to achieve success in your weight loss plan and overall health by taking an entirely different approach. Instead of demonizing fats, like many other diets do, and forcing you to resort to extreme exercise techniques, keto works by changing the fuel source the body uses to stay energized.

One reason many people love keto is because it is not complicated. Keto is easy to understand and follow. In fact, it can be done in three easy steps:

1. Significantly cut down on carbs
2. Increase your intake of healthy fats
3. Allow your body to enter ketosis and enjoy the benefits

The Keto diet has so many benefits, apart from its ability to help people lose weight significantly; research has shown this diet can help you to fight some serious diseases, including Alzheimer's and cancer.
In the next chapter, we will discuss what the keto diet is all about.

Chapter 2

WHAT IS KETOGENIC DIET?

A keto diet is a low-carb, high-fat, and adequate protein diet that forces the body to produce ketones in the liver to produce energy. Today, the ketogenic diet is known by many names. In most circles, it is known as "*keto.*" There are also people who call it low-carb diet, as well as other names, such as low-carb high-fat (LCHF) diet.

The Keto diet aims to turn the body into a fat-burning machine. As mentioned above, keto was initially developed as a treatment for epilepsy. However, it gained its recent popularity as more people began to seek new ways to burn fat faster. Apart from its fat-burning and weight-loss benefits, keto has many other proven health benefits, which include health and improved performance. We will discuss this in detail later in this book.

Here is the Logic behind Keto:
Most of us eat foods that are very high in carbs almost daily. However, what you may not know is that, whenever you eat something with high carbs content, your body will produce insulin and glucose. Now, these two nutrients are essential because:

- Glucose: Your body can easily convert glucose and use it as energy. Since glucose is the easiest molecule the human body can convert into energy, your body will easily choose this energy source over other energy sources
- Insulin: This chemical is produced to process the glucose in your bloodstream. It does its job by taking the glucose around your body to where it's needed

Now, since your body uses glucose as the primary energy source, it does not need fat; therefore, it stores it in various parts of your body. This is the reason you gain weight. The excessive fats in your waistline were probably caused by unburned fats stored there. For instance, if you eat a diet that is high in carbohydrate, your body will only use glucose as the primary energy.

The logic behind the ketogenic diet, therefore, is that you can induce your body into a state known as *"ketosis"* by lowering your intake of carbs.

What is Ketosis?

Ketosis is a biological process that takes place in the body. It is a completely natural process the body will initiate to help the body survive when the food intake is low. Whenever the body enters this natural process, it will produce a compound known as *"ketones"* from the breakdown of fats in the liver.

This ketosis happens when the liver succeeds in breaking down fat into fatty acids and glycerol.

It does this through a process known as "beta-oxidation." This activity will lead to the production of 3 types of ketone bodies that include:

- Acetoacetate
- Beta-hydroxybutyrate
- Acetone

After the production of these ketone bodies, your body will further break them into an energy-rich substance, known as "ketones", which is circulated through the bloodstream. The end result of this process is that it will alter your metabolism to access fat deposits in your body and burn them faster. Perhaps, this is the reason most people say the keto diet turns your body into a ***"fat-burning machine."*** Studies have shown that burning ketones is a much "cleaner" way to keep the body energized compared to overloading the body with carbs and sugar every day.

Hopefully, by now, the logic behind the ketogenic diet is becoming more apparent to you. We eat the keto diet to force the body to initiate this metabolic state to burn fat deposits. However, this is not done through starvation of calories but through starvation of carbohydrates.

The great thing about our bodies is they are very adaptive. In a situation where you overload your body with fats and remove carbs, your body will start to burn ketones and use it as the primary form of energy. When you achieve the optimal ketone levels, you will enjoy a host of other benefits apart from the fast fat-burning process and the subsequent weight loss.

Ketones are produced when you eat very low carbs. When you keep eating foods high in fat but low in carbs, you will force the entire body to switch its fuel supply to run almost entirely on fat. This process forces you to produce low insulin and dramatically increases the fat-burning process. During this process, your body can easily delve into the fats stored in various parts of your body and burn them as well.

The fastest way to produce ketones or force the body into this process is through fasting. Unfortunately, long-term fasting is not feasible, especially when you have work to do or children to take care of. The ketogenic diet mimics the same beneficial effects of fasting. These benefits are achieved when the body is tricked into thinking it is fasting.

How Ketosis Works:

Below, you can see the summary of how you can achieve ketosis and how it works:

1. Significantly reduce glucose from foods such as carbohydrate, grains, fruits, and other sources of sugar.
2. The first step will force the body to look for an alternative fuel source, which is fat that is converted into ketones when carbohydrates are not easily accessible.
3. The body will burn fats to produce ketones in the absence of glucose.
4. The ketone will force your body to enter a state known as ketosis.
5. Ketosis will lead to a fast fat-burning process, which further leads to quick and consistent weight loss until you can achieve a healthy, stable new body weight.

How to Achieve Ketosis

The objective of the ketogenic diet is to force the body into ketosis. It is a way of tricking the body into thinking you are fasting.

To induce ketosis, you will have to limit your intake of carbohydrates significantly. When you limit your carbs intake, you will cut off the supply of glucose to your cells. Note that carbs are not the only thing you need to cut out; you will also need to limit the consumption of protein, since protein can also be converted into glucose in small amounts. This is the difference between keto and other diets, such as Paleo and Atkins diet. These diets restrict carbs but still allow intake of protein in high volume. Thus, they don't result in ketosis.

You can make use of the ketosis food plan to achieve ketosis. You can do this by:

- Getting at least 60-80% of your daily calories from fat sources
- Getting 15-25% of calories from protein sources
- Getting 5-10% of calories from carbs

When you want to transition to ketosis, it is recommended that you aim for about 30-50 net grams of carbs. Starting with this amount of carbs is considered a flexible amount. However, you need to reduce your carb intake continually once you get used to eating this way. Cut down the number of carbs you get to about 20 grams of net carbs per day. 20 net grams of carbs is considered the *"standard"* amount that will allow you to get the best results. However, you should have it in mind that everybody is a bit different. The result you may get can differ.

Note that what the ketogenic diet considers is the net grams of carbs, not the total grams. Net grams of carbs are the number of carbs left when you have subtracted grams of fiber from total grams of carbs.

Here is an example:

If you are eating vegetables that contain total 5 grams of carbohydrates, but about 3 grams of these total grams come from fiber, your net gram of carbs is just 2 grams. This is the number you will need to add to your daily plan.

How to determine the amount of calories you need:

You can easily determine the amount of each macronutrient group per day by using an online calculator. This will help you to know precisely the number of calories you need to be eating in total to achieve weight loss or maintain the current weight you have.

Once you figure out the number of calories you need, split your calorie intake into proteins, fats, and carbs.

Once you start this process, don't forget to increase your daily intake of electrolytes. You need to get more potassium from foods like avocado and leafy greens. Finally, drink more water and always get exercise to boost your result.

Signs of Ketosis

When you start ketosis, you will notice some signs. This is because this diet, unlike some other diets, will affect your metabolism and significantly change the way it works. Ideally, it would take most people about 3-4 weeks to ease into the diet and adjust to the changes. In some cases, you may experience some adverse symptoms as a result of the early stage of ketosis.

In some quarters, these negative symptoms of ketosis are known as "the keto flu." No doubt, implementing this diet can be particularly challenging for anyone, at least for the first one to two weeks. However, these symptoms will go away once you get used to the diet. As your body gets used to being in ketosis, the symptoms will disappear.

Some Symptoms you may experience include:
- Trouble sleeping
- Feeling tired
- Low energy level
- Struggling with digestive problems, such as constipation and bloating
- Feeling weak during a workout session
- Low recovery rate after workout sessions
- Suffering from bad breath
- Loss of libido
- Easily irritable and being moodier

Do not let these negative symptoms deter you. Just like every good thing, the initial phase is usually the toughest. These symptoms mentioned above will go away once you become used to the diet. It may seem tough in the initial phase, but the good news is that you will notice improvement in several health markers once you go deeper into ketosis. After a few weeks of ketosis, you will begin to notice:

- Reduced hunger and cravings
- Weight loss
- Increased mental performance
- Improved energy
- Improvement in your mood

All these signs show the hard part is over and you are now reaping the benefits of ketosis. According to most experts, you will begin to reap the full benefits of ketosis when you have achieved an optimal ketosis level. They believe this optimal level is **between 1.5 and 3 mmol/L** (number of ketones in the blood). This is the level where you will begin to enjoy weight loss, as well as other health benefits. It is important to mention that everyone is different when it comes to the macronutrient ratio you need to stay in range and feel your best regarding levels of energy and other symptoms.

The best way to get into the optimal ketosis is to experiment with different amounts of carbs. This will help you to determine how they affect your ketone levels. You can continue experimenting to remain in nutritional ketosis level, which is about 0.5 to 3.0 mM. However, don't experiment immediately after an exercise. Get enough rest after exercise before you experiment again.

Tests to Know You Are in Ketosis

You can know you are in ketosis by using various tests available. Some of these tests include:

- **Blood Ketone Meter**

With this test, you can get the exact measurement of levels of BHB ketones in your blood. Fortunately, you can purchase this meter online. In some cases, they are a bit pricey. Check Amazon and Wal-Mart for a great deal on these meters. The great thing about these meters is they are very reliable when you want to know you are eating the right macronutrient ratio required to remain in ketosis.

- **Urine Tests**

If you cannot afford the meter recommended above, you can use inexpensive urine strip tests to know if you are in ketosis. This method is cost-effective. The only problem is it reveals just the acetoacetate ketone levels and won't show you the levels of BHB. Some popular urine strip tests you can use include Uriscan and Ketostix.

- **Breathalyzer**

This method does not require strips. This method is used to measure the ketone known as acetone. The downside is this method may not be as accurate as blood tests.

Chapter 3

BENEFITS OF KETOGENIC DIET

What Are the Benefits of the Keto Diet

The ketogenic diet has many benefits. In recent years, this diet has become popular due to a number of advantages. Below, you will learn some of the benefits of this diet:

1. Helps with Weight Loss

This is the single most important benefit of a keto diet. In fact, this is the reason most people try to achieve ketosis. When you enter ketosis, you can experience quick and substantial weight loss. This is a perfect diet for those who are overweight or obese to lose substantial weight. A study by British Journal of Nutrition revealed you can achieve better long-term body weight when you follow the keto diet. This study also showed you will be able to achieve better cardiovascular risk factor management with keto.

What makes this diet so powerful for achieving weight loss is it has a solid physiological and biochemical basis. With the low-carbs and high-fat diets, you can reduce hunger while boosting weight loss.

Moreover, foods that are high in healthy fats can be very filling. Eating such foods will give you the feeling of fullness and therefore prevent you from overeating. This can stop your cravings for foods such as sweets and junk foods, which make you gain weight.

2. Lower Your Risk of Heart Disease

According to the CDC, heart disease is one of the most common killer diseases in the United States and other developed nations. With the keto diet, you can lower the risk of heart disease markers. Some of these markers include triglycerides, as well as high cholesterol.

Even with high-fat content, this diet is unlikely to impact your cholesterol levels negatively. Alternatively, it has what it takes to reduce your cardiovascular disease risk factors, especially in people who are overweight or obese.

In a study, it was discovered that eating most of the recommended keto diet foods will help you to have decreased levels of LDL cholesterol (also known as bad cholesterol), triglycerides, and blood glucose. The study also showed you can increase the level of HDL cholesterol.

3. Lower Your Risk of Type-2 Diabetes

Today, millions of people are suffering from Type-2 diabetes in the United States. Fortunately, the keto diet is one food you can use to lower your risk of Type-2 diabetes. The Keto diet lowers your risk of diabetes by controlling the release of hormones such as insulin. These hormones play major roles in the development of Type-2 diabetes, as well as other diseases. Insulin is released when you eat carbohydrates as a reaction to elevated blood glucose.

When this happens, it signals your cells to store as much energy as possible as glycogen and later as body fat. The Keto diet helps you to eliminate carbs from your diet and therefore keep carb stores empty. You can prevent the release of too much insulin when you significantly reduce the amount of carbs you are consuming. When you keep the secretion of insulin very low, you can avoid Type-2 diabetes, which has too much insulin as a risk factor.

3. Offer Protection Against Cancer

When your body is in ketosis, it tricks the body into believing it is fasting, thus starving off certain cancer cells. A study showed that regular cells use fat for energy, but cancer cells cannot metabolically shift to use fat instead of glucose.

Studies such as the ones conducted at the National Institutes of Neurological Disorders and Stroke revealed the keto diet is an effective treatment for certain types of cancers, as well as other health problems.

4. Lower the Risk of Other Chronic Diseases

Originally, the Keto diet was developed to stop seizures and treat epilepsy. There is strong evidence that you can manage some serious diseases with keto. Some of these diseases include Parkinson's disease, Alzheimer's disease, and even some types of cancers.

Scientists are still trying to understand how the keto diet helps to treat these health problems. However, many believe that, by significantly cutting off glucose supply and putting the body in ketosis, the biological process that follows helps to prevent and eliminate short-circuits in the brain's signaling system, which causes seizures, cellular damage, as well as tumor growth.

5. Lead to Improvement in Blood Sugar Control

The benefits of the keto diet are not limited to better weight management. It is well-known that the keto diet can help you better control your blood sugar levels. Poor blood sugar control can lead to problems such as:

- Diabetes
- Heart disease
- High blood pressure
- Indigestion
- Certain types of cancer

You will be able to avoid many health problems when you have better control of your blood sugar levels.

6. High Energy Levels and Better Focus

Once your body adapts to using ketones as fuel instead of glucose, your muscles will learn how to use a ketogenic source of energy. These new energy levels will help you to accomplish many tasks during the day. Moreover, with enhanced mental focus, which you will achieve as a result of this diet, you will be more productive throughout your day.

7. Live Longer

There is evidence that suggests you may be able to extend your lifespan by simply eating a low-carb, high-fat diet instead of a low-fat diet. According to a study in the Medical Journal, "The Lancet" - over 135,000 adults from about eighteen countries of the world were observed for a number of years. At the end of the study, it was discovered that adults who were on a low-carbs, high-fat diet were able to reduce some diseases that might have affected their health and reduced their lifespan.

Types of Ketogenic Diet

When you have decided to use a ketogenic diet to achieve long-term and sustainable weight loss, you will also need to decide which type of ketogenic diet to adopt.

Fortunately, you can choose the type of ketogenic diet you want based on your needs. However, these types of keto diets share some similarities, and the underlying principle remains the same. The only difference is that some types of keto diets are easier to follow, while others are hard. It is important to note that the hard ones seem to bring results quicker.

Below, you choose the type of ketogenic diet you want to adopt.

1. Standard Ketogenic Diet (SKD)

Like the name suggests, this is the most popular type of ketogenic diet. Most people adopt this type of ketogenic diet because it is straightforward to follow.

SKD requires that you eat the minimum amount of carbs when you are following the ketogenic diet plan. You should also note this type of ketogenic diet is the same as the Atkins diet's induction phase. It contains very-low carbs, moderate protein, and high fat, i.e., 70 to 75% fat, 20% protein, and 5 to 10% carbs.

- Your grams would be:
- 40-60 grams of proteins
- 20-50 grams of carbs
- There are no set limits for fats

With this type of keto diet, you can get most of your calories from the fat in your diet. It is recommended that you add vegetables to your diet, especially non-starchy vegetables with very low carbs. If you follow this type of keto diet, it will help you lose weight, improve your heart health and blood glucose control.

2. Targeted Ketogenic Diet (TKD) - Traditional Approach

The unique thing about this approach is you will need to eat carbs at least 30-60 minutes before you start an exercise. It is recommended that you choose carbs that are easily digestible and have high Glycemic index. This is to ensure you don't suffer from stomach upset. You will also need to avoid foods with high fructose content, e.g., fruits.

You will be able to burn the carbs you eat efficiently and completely before exercising. You are required to eat between 20 and 50 grams of net carbs before exercising. When you are done with your exercises, you need to eat foods that are high in protein but low in fat. Eating fats right after exercise is not recommended because it impairs nutrient absorption and muscle recovery.

3. MCT Ketogenic Diet (MKD)

The MCT Ketogenic Diet is similar to the Standard keto diet, but it puts more focus on using medium chain triglycerides (MCT) to provide the fat required by the body.

MCTs are considered good fat, and they can be found in coconut oil. In the past, the MCT keto diet has been used as a treatment for epilepsy. MCT is recommended because it provides more ketones per gram of fat. Note that side-effects of MCTs include stomach upset and diarrhea, especially when you consume it in large amount on its own. To avoid this side effect, it is recommended that you balance your meal with MCTs and non-MCT fat.

4. Cyclic Ketogenic Diet (CKD)

The Cyclic ketogenic diet has one underlying principle; it recommends alternating ketogenic diet days with days of carb-loading, which means days of high-carb consumption. A day of carb-loading typically lasts 24-48 hours.

You will need about 50 grams of carbs per day during the first phase of carb-loading. During the carb-loading phase, you will need about 450-600 grams of carbs. You can use this type of diet to achieve fast fat loss, while building lean mass. This keto diet is mostly recommended for bodybuilders and athletes and is not for everyone.

Chapter 4

KETO DIET PLAN

The next step after becoming familiar with the types of keto diets is the Keto diet plan. The Keto diet plan is a plan that allows you to limit your carbohydrate intake to about 20-30 net grams daily.

Note: Net grams of carb is just the carb remaining after you have taken dietary fiber into account. The best keto diet is the one that accounts for dietary fiber. If you are missing this point, you need to correct it as soon as possible, so you can enjoy the full benefits of a keto diet.

When choosing the type of keto diet you want to adopt or diet plan you want to follow, you need to consider a number of factors, including gender, age, current job, current body composition, and even your level of daily activities.

How much Protein is Too Much for Keto?

If you choose the "standard Keto" or any other type of keto, make sure you account for the amount of protein you are getting. Unlike other foods, protein is not a big part of keto. This is because your body can change protein to glucose in small amounts. This means you need to limit your protein intake significantly to avoid slowing down your body's transition to ketosis. Ideally, I would recommend you keep your protein intake between

1 and 1.5 grams per kilograms of your body weight. A way to convert pounds to kilograms is to divide your ideal body weight by 2.2. For instance, as a woman weighing about 150 pounds (i.e., 68 kilograms), you will need about 68-102 grams of protein per day.

Don't forget you will need to get a lot of water daily. You need water to stay hydrated and avoid feeling fatigued. Moreover, water will help you to suppress hunger and improve digestion. It is also essential for the detoxification of your body. You will need to get about 10-12 glasses of water every day whether you are following the keto diet plan or not.

Keto Diet List: What You Can Eat or Not Eat

To know exactly what to eat and what you should avoid, you will need to understand the underlying principle of keto diet - it is simple: "Keep your carbs down and your fats high." If you are hoping to lose weight or improve your overall health with a keto diet, this list will help you to understand the foods you should eat and those you will need to avoid.

Here is what to eat:

You need meals with high healthy fat content. The fat in your meal should make up to 80% of your total calories. You can get healthy fats from foods such as coconut oil, olive oil, palm oil, grass-fed butter, seeds, and even from some nuts. Without a doubt, fats are a vital part of the ketogenic recipe. You need it to provide the body an alternative energy source, prevent hunger and fatigue. However, you need to make sure you are choosing only the healthy fats to enjoy the best benefits of keto without complicating your health.

You need non-starchy vegetables in your keto meals. Unfortunately, most people don't know this. The good thing about non-starchy vegetables is that you won't need to worry about increasing your carb intake too much. Some of these vegetables include broccoli and cruciferous veggies. You should also try all types of leafy greens, such as cucumber, asparagus, and zucchini; they are known to be non-starchy.

Finally, you will need to add foods that are high in protein but contain low or no carbohydrates. Some of these foods include wild-caught fish, cage-free eggs, grass-fed meat, organ meats, and even some full-fat dairy products are in this category.

Foods to avoid:

You will need to avoid foods that are high in carbs. Do away with those foods you are used to before starting your keto diet. Some of these foods include processed foods, fruits, and drinks that are high in sugar, as well as many other high-carb foods.

Best Keto Foods

Below are some foods sources you need to eat when you are following the Keto diet. These foods include:

Healthy Fats

Healthy fats contain zero net carbs. I have listed some of these healthy fats below. Remember you need to include a high amount of fats to your food every day.

Some good examples of healthy fats include:

- Saturated Fats
- Monounsaturated fats
- Some types of polyunsaturated fats (Omega-3 fatty acids)
- MCT Oil from palm fruit, cold-pressed coconut, olive oil, macadamia, flaxseed, and avocado oil
- Butter and ghee
- Chicken fat, duck fat, lard

Proteins

You will need protein in your foods but not in a large amount. When it comes to a keto diet, animal proteins from sources such as fish and meat are mostly preferred because they have little or no carbs.

You will need to eat these proteins in a moderate amount, so you can control hunger. When you are choosing your meat, choose fattier cuts, instead of leaner ones. For instance, instead of choosing chicken breast, choose chicken thighs and legs.

Some good examples of good proteins to include in your keto diet include:

- Grass-fed meat (Veal, goat, lamb, venison) - they are high in quality omega-3 fats and have 0 grams of net carbs per 5 ounces
- Organ meats (liver) - they contain about 3 grams net carbs per 5 ounces
- Poultry such as quail, chicken, turkey, hen, pheasant, duck, and goose. They are good because they have 0 grams net carb per 5 ounces
- Cage-free eggs - they only contain 1 gram net carb each
- Fish such as trout, tuna, bass, anchovies, salmon, flounder, mackerel, and sardines - they contain about 0 grams of net carbs per 5 ounces

Non-Starchy Vegetables

Non-starchy vegetables are great for your keto diet. We recommend you get them from the following sources:

- Cruciferous veggies such as cabbage, broccoli, cauliflower, and Brussels sprouts - for just 1 cup, you will get 3-6 grams net carbs
- All leafy greens such as mustard, beet greens, dandelion, turnip, endive, chicory, arugula, radicchio, fennel, escarole, spinach, sorrel, romaine, collards, chard, kale - these

goods have about 0.5 - 5 net carbs per 1 cup
- Fresh herbs - almost to net gram carbs per 1-2 tablespoons
- Celery, zucchini, cucumber, leeks, and chives - you get about 2-4 grams net carbs per 1 cup

Fat-Based Fruit

- Avocado contains 3.7 net gram carbs per half

Snacks

- Hard-boiled eggs - just one gram net carb
- Bone broth - contains 0 grams net carbs per serving
- Half avocado with sliced salmon - this has about 3-4 grams net carbs
- Minced meat wrapped in lettuce - contains about 1 gram net carbs

Condiments

- Apple cider vinegar - has about 1 gram net carbs

- Unsweetened mustard - contains about 0-1 grams net carbs
- Hot sauce without any sweetener- no carbs
- Herbs - no carbs

Drinks

- Water - no carbs
- Bone broth - no carbs
- Unsweetened black coffee and tea - no carbs

Foods You Should Never Eat

Avoid All Types of Sugar

You need to avoid every type of sugar. With one teaspoon of sugar, you will get about 4 net grams of carbs and 12 net grams of carbs with 1 tablespoon of sugar.

Avoid:
- Brown, white, raw, Caine, and confectioner's sugar
- Syrups such as carob, maple, caramel, corn, and fruit
- Agave and honey
- Foods produced with ingredients such as maltose, glucose, fructose, lactose, and dextrose

Avoid All Types of Grains

You should avoid grains like the plague when you are following the keto diet. Eating even one slice of bread can give you anywhere from 10 to 30 net grams of carbs. For example, you will get about 15-35 net gram carbs per 1/4 cup of cereals and cooked grains.

Avoid:

- Oats, wheat, pilaf, quinoa, couscous, and all rice
- Avoid everything corn and their products, such as popcorn, grits, tortillas, polenta, and cornmeal
- Products made with flour, such as rolls, bagels, bread, pasta, and muffins

Avoid Almost All Processed Foods

Most processed foods are bad for you. Avoid foods such as:

- Chips, pretzels, crackers
- Every type of candy
- Every kind of dessert, such as ice cream, pies, cookies, cakes
- Waffles, pancakes, and most baked breakfast foods
- Cereals and oatmeal
- Granola bars, snack carbs, and most protein bars
- Boxed foods, canned soups, and prepackaged meal
- Foods with artificial ingredients, such as artificial sweeteners

Avoid Sweetened and Caloric Beverages

- Alcohol
- Soda
- Fruit juices
- Milk
- Diary replacements, such as coconut, almond, soy, cow's milk, cream, half and a half
- Sweetened teas
- Sweetened coffee drinks

Recipes

Now that we've got the knowledge out of the way and you are ready to explore a keto diet, in this section I will introduce you to a colorful selection of ketogenic delicacies, it's time for us to explore just how diverse your menu can be while you achieve ketosis. For that, we will go through the day together with these recommended recipes which we will split into Breakfast, Lunch and Dinner. Let's start it off with our favorite meal of the day.

BREAKFAST

Breakfast is as we all know a very important meal, it gets you up and ready for the day after a long slumber. Our bodies wake up ready to refuel, so eating a proper ketogenic snack helps you avoid those groggy headaches and other undesirable feelings while keeping your weight in check. It's common to deprioritize or forget it in a busy morning if you are leading a busy life, but if you are committed to living healthy, this is one meal you can't ignore, and I'll help you prepare seven fun and spontaneous breakfast meals to kickstart your day.

Poppy Seed Low Carb Bread

The foundation of a breakfast starts with tasty slice of bread to compliment a clear majority of breakfast meals. One slice of low carb bread contains nearly 3.5g of carbohydrates making it ideal for bread lovers.

Preparation Time	Servings	Calories Per Slice
15 minutes, 1-hour total	10 slices	120 calories

Ingredients:

- 5 Eggs, **separated** (yolks and whites)
- 2 Eggs whole
- 200g (2 cups) Almond flour or coconut flour
- 1 pinch of salt
- ¼ teaspoon All-Natural Cream of Tartar
- 80g Avocado or olive oil
- 1 tablespoon Baking powder
- 1 tablespoon Poppy seeds

Preparation

01 We start by preheating our oven to 180C (356°).
02 Prepare a large loaf baking bowl by placing a slice of baking paper only covering the bottom of it so our bread doesn't stick after baking.
03 Prepare two large bowls for mixing.

04 Crack open 5 eggs separating the whites in a bowl and the yolks in different one.

05 Crack open your remaining 2 eggs and add them to the yolk bowl.

06 Add the avocado or olive oil to yolk bowl.

07 Whisk until you reach a smooth consistency.

08 To this mixture you can now add the baking powder and a pinch of salt, and 2 cups of Almond flour.

09 Mix everything very well with a wooden spoon or a spatula.

10 Start working on the egg whites bowl by adding the cream of tartar to it and the poppy seeds into the mixture if you want them inside your bread, if not you can simply add them to the top of your loaf (bottom of your baking pan).

11 Whisk this mixture very well until it's smooth preferably with an electric whisk.

12 Transfer the mixture to the yolk bowl and thoroughly but softly mix everything together until no white lines are visible.

13 Pour your delicious looking batter into the baking bowl and when done smooth out the surface using your spatula (or spoon).

14 Bake this delicacy for 35-45 minutes depending on your oven. In the mid-section of your oven.

15 Make sure you check on it frequently to make sure that it has formed a beautiful golden crust.

16 Once that's done take it out of the oven and leave it for 5-10 minutes to cool off, so it'll be easier to remove it from the baking bowl.

17 Using a thin knife cut along the edges of the bowl and remove your bread.

18 Let your loaf cool down in room temperature covered by a cloth for 15-20 minutes before you slice it up and serve it.

19 Enjoy!

This delicacy goes well with a myriad of other meals, it is the foundation of a keto breakfast as you'll notice how your sandwiches not only taste better than white bread but also are healthier. Naturally, this low carb bread should be prepared the night before consumption because let's face it, who has time to bake for an hour every day before work.

Avocado Sunrise

Nothing soothes our breakfast thirst more than a cool, tasty smoothie to start off the day. Whether you're going out on your morning run or simply wish to start your day with a little nutritious kick, this detoxifying, dairy-free smoothie will make you feel full while going easy on your tummy. It's rich in antioxidants and anti-inflammatory agents and just the right hint of ginger to make you come back for more.

Preparation Time	Servings	Calories Per Slice
10-15 minutes	2 smoothies	240 calories

Ingredients:

- 1 cup Coconut milk (canned)
- ¼ cup Almond milk
- ½ Avocado
- 2 tablespoons turmeric
- 1 tablespoon fresh ginger
- 1-2 tablespoons of squeezed lime juice depending on taste
- 1 cup of crushed ice
- 1-3 teaspoon of honey

Preparation

01 Fairly easy to prepare, you will naturally need a blender for this- or any other smoothie you make. Just add everything except the ice and honey and gradually mix on low-speed.
02 Once your smoothie isn't chunky, you can add the crushed ice and gradually put teaspoons of honey.
03 Mix on high-speed.
04 Taste it and check if it needs more honey.
05 If the mixture is too thick for your taste, you can add a little bit of water to even it out. Better yet coconut water. If the mixture is too thin, you can strengthen it and make it thicker with a slice of frozen banana, entirely optional.
06 Enjoy!

This smoothie goes well with low carb biscuits, but normally the avocado sunrise alone consists a full breakfast. A note to my dear reader: go easy on the ginger and turmeric, while they are amazingly healthy they can ruin the taste of a smoothie if overused.

Brussels Sprout American Breakfast

What constitutes a quintessential, traditional American breakfast is a combination of eggs, bacon, and a catalyst in between. This meal is simply a variation or alternate way of preparing that breakfast in a way to better fit the keto diet. While I chose brussels sprouts because they contain a very high level of vitamins, you may also substitute it with equally nutritious zucchini or broccoli based on your favorite vegetable. This meal also constitutes a full breakfast although I found it to go very well with the keto bread. This, however, depends on your daily intake target.

Preparation Time	Servings	Calories Per Slice
25 minutes total	1	676 Calories

Ingredients:

- 200g thoroughly washed Brussel Sprouts
- 60g Bacon, high fat
- 1.5 tablespoon Coconut oil
- ½ White onion
- ½ Garlic clove
- 1.5 tablespoon Freshly cut parsley, do not use packaged, must be fresh
- 1 Egg
- 1 pinch Black pepper spice

Preparation

01 Using a cutting board first we peel, cut and chop the onion into small pieces.
02 Cut the garlic clove into tiny pieces. The idea is that it melts in the pan later.
03 Cut the bacon into small bite-sized pieces.
04 Put your favorite pan on medium heat and add the oil to it.
05 Place the garlic, onion, and bacon into the oiled pan and cook them until they are browned. Make sure you don't burn the onions.
06 Make sure you prewash your brussels sprouts, and they are now dry, then cut each piece in half.
07 Add them to the pan. Note: Make sure they don't contain water to avoid dangerous reactions with oil.
08 Cook everything for 15 minutes.
09 When everything is cooked and smelling delicious place them in a small bowl, make sure you don't transfer the oil with it as you do so, if it hasn't dried already.
10 Sprinkle a pinch of black pepper over the mix.
11 Whisk 1 egg and fry it quickly in the same pan. Don't season the egg at all.
12 Place the fried egg on top of your mix in the bowl.
13 Add the freshly cut parsley on top.
14 Enjoy!

This is a favorite of mine because it can have many variations depending on the tastes of the reader, you may replace the green element in it with your favorite vegetable of choice as eggs and bacon work well with many of them. I have tried it with spinach, zucchini, mushrooms, and broccoli and it kept getting better and better.

Keto Baba Ghanoush with Flatbread

Chances are you came across baba ghanoush at some point in your life. If you haven't then I'm proud to be the first to introduce you to this delicious middle eastern appetizer that can constitute a full breakfast when combined with flatbread or sliced carrots. It is more of a dip, but a delicious eggplant based dip which is low carb, rich in antioxidants and incredibly healthy. This meal requires moderate kitchen time and skill, but I promise you'll be addicted after you try just one bite.

 Preparation Time 1-hour for Baba ghanoush, 25 for flatbread. 1.5 hours total	 Servings 6 flatbread slices, 6 servings Baba ghanoush
 Calories per flatbread slice 144 Calories	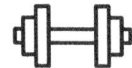 Calories per Baba Ghanoush 330 Calories

Ingredients for flatbread:

- ¼ tablespoon Garlic powder
- 2 tablespoons almond flour (specifically this flour)
- 1 Egg
- 1 tablespoon Cream cheese
- ½ cup grated aged mozzarella (low moisture)
- 1 pinch of Salt
- ¼ cup cooked and water/moisture drained Spinach

Preparation

01 Preheat your oven to 180C (356°).
02 Using a microwave (if available) place the cream cheese into a bowl which can be used in microwaves along with the grated mozzarella and melt them together. Carefully check on the mixture every now and then to make sure it doesn't clump. You need to stir it regularly between microwaving until they are melted and mixed properly.
03 Take the bowl out and mix in it the egg, the drained spinach, and the almond flour.
04 Mix thoroughly but don't take too long or the cheese will work against you.
05 Cover a baking pan with a sheet of baking paper.
06 Pour the mixture on top of it and flatten it with a spatula or spoon.
07 Add the pinch of salt and garlic powder.
08 Place it in the middle section (rack) of the oven and bake it for 15-20 minutes. Once that's done flip it over and bake the underside for about 3 minutes just enough to give it a crisp.
09 You can bake it for a longer time if you want the bread to be crispier.
10 Enjoy!

Note: Do not attempt to skip roasting the eggplant as it will not result in a baba ghanoush, rather something you really don't want to eat. Make sure that it's properly roasted and creamy before you mix it.

Ingredients for Baba ghanoush:

- 4 large Italian eggplants (male). When buying eggplants look at the bottom side of the vegetable, do you see that indentation? Do you notice that they differ? Some are slanted, some are circled almost like dots. What you want is 4 dotted ones because those are male eggplants and they won't have messy seeds to make the dip bitter like the female ones (slanted) do. You learned it first here
- 3 Garlic cloves crushed
- 1 tablespoon Salt (you can add later if you need to)
- 2.5 tablespoons of chopped parsley
- 3 tablespoons of avocado or olive oil
- 3 tablespoon Tahini (the secret ingredient)
- ½ tablespoon cayenne
- 2 tablespoons of Greek yogurt (plain)
- 1 pinch dry mint
- Lemon juice from 1 whole lemon

Preparation

01 Preheat oven to 200C (400°).
02 Careful when handling oven. Just a reminder.
03 Slice and throw away the stem and bottom section of the eggplants.
04 Slice the eggplants into disk shapes and place them on top of a parchment paper in the oven tray. But don't place it in the oven just yet!

05 Sprinkle salt on them and let the salt take away the moisture for about 25 minutes.
06 Using a knife slash the surface of the disks a couple of times, make an X mark on each disk.
07 Dab the eggplant slices in paper towels to remove water.
08 Seeing as this is a messy dish you'll need to repeat step 7 a couple of times making sure they don't have any extra water.
09 Place them back on the parchment paper which is on the oven tray and put that into your top section (rack) of your oven and roast them for 5-10 minutes.
10 Careful as eggplants roast fast and easily, you don't want the baba ghanoush to taste burnt.
11 Take out of the oven and carefully remove the skin. Some leave the skin at this point, but I recommend peeling it as it is the tradition.
12 Now you have a choice to make, you can either put the peeled and cooked eggplant slices into a blender, or you can use a bowl and mix them manually with a rough object like a whisk. I recommend the whisk.
13 Add the crushed garlic, salt, parsley, olive oil, tahini, cayenne, yogurt, dry mint, and lemon juice to the bowl (or blender) and mix thoroughly.
14 Just when you thought the mixing is over, you need to mix and whisk it some more as this dip needs a lot of work to be properly ready. (Alternatively, you could blend it on high speed until it's done).
15 Take the mixture and pour it into a bowl.
16 Decorate it accordingly with dry mint, olive oil, sliced tomatoes and whole mint leaves.
17 Enjoy!

If you've made it this far in the Baba Ghanoush and Flatbread cooking, then you deserve to spoil your self to one of the most popular and delicious ketogenic breakfasts available. It might be a lot of work, but you can't deny that dipping that spinach flatbread slice in it and having a bite doesn't taste amazing. I also recommend that you cool the Baba Ghanoush in a refrigerator for about 15-20 minutes before serving as it intensifies the tastes. Alternatively, you could slice up some carrots and dip them in it as well if the flatbread isn't suitable. Whatever you do, remember that while tahini is the secret ingredient here, too much of it can make the dip a little too dense so keep to 3 tablespoons.

Scallion Halloumi American Breakfast

Traditionally nothing says breakfast better than a frying pan, eggs and a secret ingredient that gives a person an optimistic start to a brand-new day. This meal, however, takes it a whole new level with the Halloumi cheese. As far back as medieval Egypt halloumi was munched on by the Mediterranean people. Currently considered as a Cypriot tradition this cheese is fried and served due to its high melting point. Combine that with scallion, eggs, and bacon, and you have yourself an amazing meal.

Preparation Time	Servings	Calories Per Serving
30 minutes total	2	580 Calories

Ingredients:

- Salt, variable to taste
- Black pepper, variable to taste. (Don't overdo this)
- 2 Scallions
- 5 eggs
- 120g Bacon
- 80g Halloumi
- 6 tablespoons Parsley (fresh)
- 6 tablespoons pitted black olives. (avoid green olives with this meal)
- 2.5 tablespoons Olive oil or Avocado oil
- 3 tablespoons Coriander, chopped fresh leaves

Preparation

01 Using a cutting board dice the halloumi well into equal sized cubes.
02 Slice the bacon and dice it to almost the same size as the halloumi cubes.
03 Slice each olive in half, tedious but necessary.
04 Finely dice the scallions into little bites.
05 Lather a frying pan with avocado oil or olive oil and set it on medium heat.
06 Don't overdo it with the oil, just enough to fry the halloumi, bacon, and scallions.
07 Fry them until they are brown and cooked.
08 While you did all that, you would have whisked the parsley, coriander, eggs, black pepper, and salt.
09 Pour the whisked mixture on top of the frying pan. (on the halloumi, bacon and scallion mix).
10 Add the sliced olives and stir until your meal is nice and ready.
11 Enjoy with a cup of tea.

This is a slight variation of the usual eggs and bacon breakfast. But, the scallion and coriander will give you a noticeable change and finally the halloumi contrasts so well with bacon that I just can't get enough of it. The ingredients can be changed slightly if you wish you can add diced tomatoes, or instead of scallions and coriander you can use fresh whole spinach leaves (not frozen). You may also use feta instead of halloumi, just remember not to fry the feta rather just add it as a final ingredient to your plate.

Raspberry Pecan Pancake

Truly the beauty of pancakes isn't the fact that you have a wide range of toppings that compliment them. It's the fact that everyone loves them. No breakfast list is complete without at least one mention of them, and youngsters would much rather have them for breakfast than any other meal. So, without further ado here's our ketogenic variation of pancakes.

Preparation Time	Servings	Calories Per Serving
30 minutes total	12 pancakes	286 Calories

Ingredients:

- ¼ tablespoon Salt
- 2 tablespoons Vanilla extract
- 1.5 cup Almond flour
- 2 tablespoon Erythritol
- 1 pinch Cinnamon
- 1 teaspoon Baking powder
- 6 Eggs
- 8 tablespoons Almond or Coconut milk
- Raspberries depending on how many you want
- 1 tablespoon Butter (unsalted)
- 60g chopped Pecans

Preparation

01 You need a large bowl for this delicacy.
02 Whisk the almond flour, vanilla extract, the almond milk, erythritol, and cinnamon together (leave some cinnamon for later).
03 Crack open the eggs and add to mix.
04 Whisk thoroughly.
05 Add the salt and baking powder.
06 Check to see if consistency is suitable, if it's thick and heavy you can add a little bit of coconut or almond milk depending on which you used in step 2.
07 Place your favorite pancake pan on the stove and preheat it (a coat of olive oil is essential).
08 Slowly pour the pancake mix to form a beautiful circle.
09 Let it fry for about 2 minutes until it inflates and bubbles up.
10 Flip and cook the underside.
11 Make sure it's browned to your desire and repeat with the rest of the pancake mixture until you are done.
12 Using the same pan drop the chopped pecans and toast just a little bit. Be very careful not to overdo it.
13 Use leftover cinnamon from step 2 and sprinkle on top of pecan.
14 Add Raspberries.
15 Add any desired toppings to your pancakes and roll them into pancake "Cigars".
16 Refrigerate for 15 minutes.
17 Enjoy!

As I mentioned, one of the greatest things about pancakes is that you can add almost any topping you can imagine. If you're following a keto safe-list, you're good to go. One variation is to add fresh mint leaves to the rolls, but it might not appeal to everybody.

Coriander Shakshouka

The Middle Eastern cuisine is ripe with exotic dishes that frankly don't get the attention they deserve, a prime example is the shakshouka, a much-enjoyed breakfast in Israel and the Levant area. While recipes vary from country to country, I found it's easy to make, simple, and most importantly fits right into a keto breakfast

Preparation Time	Servings	Calories Per Serving
25-30 minutes total	6	318 Calories

Ingredients:

- 1 large diced Red pepper
- 400g ground spicy Italian Sausage
- 1.5 tablespoon Coconut or avocado oil
- 1.5 tablespoon minced Garlic
- 5 Eggs
- 70g crumbled Feta cheese
- ½ diced white Onion
- 1 tablespoon Chili powder
- 60g chopped fresh Coriander
- 600g diced Tomatoes (canned, with the juice)
- 1/4 tablespoon Salt
- ¾ tablespoon Black pepper
- ½ tablespoon powdered Cumin

Preparation

01 You need a large frying pan.
02 Let's start by putting the avocado or coconut oil in the pan over medium heat.
03 Make sure the Italian sausage is ground, then add it to the pan and using a spatula mash it around and crumble it.
04 Once it's brown and cooked place the meat in a bowl (Don't take the oil with it) and put the pan back on heat.
05 Add the already diced red pepper, garlic, salt, black pepper, chili powder, onion, and cook them well. You will know when the onion has become soft.
06 Put the Italian sausage in the bowl back into the pan and pour the canned tomatoes into the mix. Stir the mixture and cook it well for about 10 minutes, or until your mixture is more pasty than saucy. You will want it to be almost dry but still mushy.
07 Using a large tablespoon, you will make 5 circles in the mixture where you can pour a cracked egg in. Press the spoon down and make a bed for each egg.
08 Once you have 5 places you can fill, crack open the eggs and pour them (white and yolk) into each bed.
09 Leave on heat until the eggs are cooked completely.
10 Now it's time to add the coriander, feta crumbs, and cumin on top.
11 Cook for about 2 more minutes and serve.
12 Enjoy!

Traditionally, you would have served this recipe with flatbread or pita, but you can get as creative as you'd like with the side dish since shakshouka can be enjoyed with any kind of bread, just make sure it's a bread made with almond flour and contains no carbs. Also, you may want to replace the Italian Sausage with another base if you're a vegetarian, however you cook it, make sure you complement it with Coriander and Feta as those are our secret ingredients for this delicacy.

LUNCH

Maintaining a diet can be at times exhausting, the reason being that we change our eating habits for the greater good of our body. We might not have the time or the patience to cook elaborate recipes, and when we do, it's possible that our expectations aren't met. The beauty of a ketogenic cuisine is how versatile and simple it is to cook highly delicious meals while still eating healthy. Reaching ketosis with these lunches will be easy, and you'll easily find yourself wondering why you didn't start earlier since your meals will be healthier, tastier, and easier to prepare. Here I will list seven of my favorite lunch recipes that will surprise you, they are so good you'll make them a home tradition.

Steamed Chicken Breast with Vegetables

Let's start off our lunch selection with a classic pan of chicken breasts and assorted vegetables, mainly because it's the healthiest way to eat chicken and it is quite simple to make, all you need is parchment paper and your favorite keto veggies to make a truly filling and nutritious meal.

Preparation Time	Servings	Calories Per Serving
15 minutes preparation, 1-hour total	4	775 Calories

Ingredients:

- 4 large boneless Chicken breasts
- Broccoli, quantity variable to preference
- Zucchini, quantity variable to preference
- Cauliflower, quantity variable to preference
- Radish, quantity variable to preference
- 4 garlic cloves (one for each chicken breast)
- Coconut oil
- 1 tablespoon Salt
- 1 tablespoon Black pepper
- 1.5 tablespoons Parsley (dry)
- 1 tablespoon fresh Dili (washed thoroughly)
- 1 tablespoon dried Mint
- 1 tablespoon dry oregano

Preparation

01 You need a large oven pan and parchment paper (no grease).
02 Preheat your oven to 180C (356°).
03 Wash the vegetables thoroughly and place in large mixing bowl.
04 Wash the breasts and deskin them (if the skin is there).
05 Using a knife cut open lines into chick breasts but don't go through, just enough to season inside it.
06 Apply the salt, black pepper, parsley, Dili, mint to the breasts and rub the spices into the breasts well.
07 Prepare the garlic cloves by skinning them and placing one inside each chicken breast where you earlier made lines add oregano as well.
08 Cover the chicken breasts and let them marinate in the spices for about 10 minutes.
09 Bring your vegetable bowl and sprinkle a little bit of dry mint and oregano.
10 Prepare a parchment paper large enough to contain the vegetables and the chicken breasts on your oven pan.
11 First place the vegetables inside it, then place the chicken breasts on top.
12 Using a brush or spoon, apply coconut oil (just a little bit) on top of the chicken breasts and spread evenly on their top surface.
13 Wrap the parchment paper around the whole meal (takes some practice but make sure it is completely sealed).
14 Poke 2-3 holes on top.
15 Place pan in mid-section of the oven and leave for 40 minutes.
16 Check if everything is cooked well by slightly opening the parchment paper and checking the breasts for that rich brown color.
17 Take out of the oven and let it cool down for 5 minutes.

18 Serve with avocado sauce or any sauce of your preference (keto sauces only!).
19 Enjoy!

This is our favorite pan meal, it's unbelievably easy to make, and almost any salad you can think of can complement it. It's great as an evening leftover-snack. You can replace the vegetables with your favorites. Just avoid potatoes and carrots for obvious reasons (carbs).

Keto Chicken Salad

Salads for lunch are usually disappointing, you finish your meal feeling like you haven't quite hit the spot, and most times a few hours later you are still feeling the urge to eat something again. Not with this dish, where most salads fail, this one will leave you happy, full, and still light and fresh enough to go about your day. It doesn't bloat you, and best of all it goes well with other dishes if you have visitors over or preparing a large feast.

Preparation Time	Servings	Calories Per Serving
10 minutes preparation, 1-hour total	4	510 Calories

Ingredients:

- 8 baby Tomatoes chopped into quarters
- 4 full Lettuce leaves, chopped
- 12 Black olives (pitted and sliced)
- ½ large Cucumber peeled and diced
- 1 Lemon (juice)
- 4 Chicken breasts, boneless and skinned
- 140g Feta cheese, diced into cubes
- 4 Chives, diced
- Arugula (rocket), quantity variable to preference
- 3 tablespoon Olive oil
- 1.5 teaspoons Salt
- 1 teaspoon Black pepper
- 2 teaspoons dry Mint (secret ingredient)

- 1 tablespoon Italian seasoning (dry oregano, dry marjoram, dry basil, dry rosemary, dry thyme, and if the available dry sage, usually they all come together as "Italian Seasoning," but you can make it if not)
- ½ teaspoon Sumac

Preparation

01 Wash all the vegetables and the breasts thoroughly.
02 Preheat your oven to 180C (356°).
03 Place your chicken breasts in a bowl and add the Italian dressing.
04 Coat the chicken breasts with 2 tablespoons of olive oil.
05 Don't forget to cut a few lines in the breasts using a knife.
06 Apply a ½ teaspoon of salt and 1 teaspoon of black pepper on chicken breasts.
07 Mix the spices well into the meat.
08 Place the chicken into oven preferably on the grilling rack in the mid-section and let them cook for about half an hour.
09 Chop, dice, and otherwise prep the salad in a bowl (all the vegetables).
10 Add the feta cheese, olive oil, squeezed lemon juice, and the remaining salt and mint.
11 Do not add black pepper to the salad.
12 Wait for the chicken to brown well, then flip them upside down and cook the underside.
13 Once the chicken is done, take out of oven and slice into little cubes.
14 Put into the salad and mix well.

15 Sprinkle the sumac on top.
16 Enjoy!

You can alternatively exclude the chicken breast and consider this a keto side dish to go with most other meals. Also, it's worth noting that I chose cucumbers you can replace those with avocados. The feta can also be excluded if you are avoiding dairy products. No matter how you make it if you followed my seasoning advice you can't go wrong with this salad.

Spicy Cauliflower and Lamb

What do you get when you combine Greek cuisine, cauliflower, and delicious lamb meat? A fantastic dish for all times of the day, but I chose this one for lunch because our spicy lamb meatballs are nutritious and filling enough to keep you steady through ketosis.

Preparation Time	Servings	Calories Per Serving
45 minutes total cooking time	4	440 Calories

Ingredients:

- 500g ground Lamb meat
- 300g Cauliflower (large heads)
- 1 teaspoon spicy Chili (powder)
- 2 teaspoon Salt, depending on taste
- 1 teaspoon Black pepper, depending on taste
- 1 teaspoon Rosemary
- 1.5 teaspoon Oregano
- 1 teaspoon garlic powder
- 1 Egg
- 3 tablespoons Avocado oil
- 1 chopped white Onion
- Mint leaves, variable to servings and taste
- 150g Feta cheese. (or another goat cheese)
- Fresh Dili leaves

Preparation

01 Wash the cauliflower and pulse it in a blender or food processor well.
02 Place a frying pan on medium heat and add 1 tablespoon of avocado oil.
03 Once the cauliflower has the same consistency as rice, move it to the pan and cook it for about 10 minutes. (add the salt and pepper to taste at this stage).
04 Set aside once cooked.
05 Prepare a mixing bowl, crack open the egg and place it inside (white and yolk, whole) and put the lamb meat, chili, salt, black pepper, rosemary, oregano, and garlic powder and mix thoroughly.
06 Once everything is mixed, pour the slightest bit of olive oil into your hands and form meatballs.
07 You can add almond flour (optional) if you feel like your meatballs aren't holding, but they will.
08 Make about 12-14 meatballs.
09 Put the remaining avocado oil in a pan and brown the onion in it.
10 Once the onion is ready, start cooking the meatballs in the same pan until they are firm and well cooked.
11 When the meatballs are done, place them on the cauliflower serving plates and decorate with mint and Dili leaves.
12 Sprinkle the feta cubes on top.
13 Serve hot.
14 Enjoy!

This cauliflower dish is usually served with dressing or sauce, but I found that most dressings take away the earthy taste of lamb and the rich punch of feta. However, if you find a little dry to your taste, you can introduce a keto sauce of your choice to go with it.

Cauliflower and Chicken Thigh Bowl

Didn't have enough of the delicious cauliflower-rice, I thought so! Cauliflower is in the very foundation of a keto diet, along with avocados. This dish brings an Asian punch with a myriad of spices, while also keeping your intake healthy and low-carb. Additionally, today you're going to learn how to make proper chick stock!

Preparation Time	Servings	Calories Per Serving
30 minutes for chicken stock, 2-hours total	6	552 Calories

Ingredients for Chicken stock:

- 400g Chicken bones
- Bunch of bay leaves
- 1 Cinnamon stick
- 4 peeled Garlic cloves
- 1 whole white Onion (chopped in half)
- ½ teaspoon Salt

Ingredients for the main dish:

- 200g Cauliflower (large heads)
- 1kg Chicken thighs (skinned, boneless)
- 6 baby tomatoes (sliced into quarters)
- 300ml Chicken stock
- 500g Coconut milk
- 3 Garlic cloves diced
- 1 whole white Onion, diced
- 2 squeezed medium Limes
- 4 chili peppers (small, diced)
- ¼ teaspoon Salt (chicken stock already salty)
- ½ teaspoon Black pepper
- 1.5 tablespoon water
- 3 teaspoons Coriander powder
- 1.5 teaspoon Cumin
- 2 teaspoons Curry powder
- 1 teaspoon Rosemary
- 2.5 tablespoons avocado or olive oil

Preparation

01 We have to put in a lot of work to do on this one, first prepare a large pot to boil the chicken legs.
02 Fill three-quarters of it with water.
03 Set to high heat, let it boil.
04 Drop the chicken bones and all the ingredients for the stock.
05 Make sure the garlic cloves are peeled before you do that.
06 Let it boil for 4 minutes, then set to medium and forget about it for 15 minutes.

07 Stir slightly and taste, add salt or pepper accordingly.
08 Take it off heat, remove ingredients and place the stock aside for later. (This is an excellent stock to cook other things with as well).
09 Cut the chicken thighs into small pieces.
10 Prepare a blender.
11 Add onion, garlic, lime juice, peppers, salt, black pepper, water, coriander, cumin, curry, and rosemary and blend them until they become pasty.
12 Oil up a deep pan (large) with either avocado or olive oil.
13 Place your mix from the blender into the pan.
14 Cook for about 10 minutes, then add the chicken thighs to the paste.
15 Add baby tomatoes and pour in the chicken stock.
16 Stir thoroughly.
17 Add coconut milk and set to medium heat.
18 Check occasionally if the chicken is well cooked, stir frequently.
19 Finally taste and add salt and black pepper accordingly.
20 Serve with cauliflower rice on the side.
21 Enjoy!

While excessive in spices, this meal when done just right can surprise you. The cinnamon from the chicken stock is noticeable, as is the hint of lime. This is by far the tastiest dish I've tried with the cauliflower rice, and I'm sure you'll love exploring it with other parts of chicken as well (breasts can substitute the thighs here if chopped into little bites)

Spicy Cheeseburgers with Eggplants

Almost everyone loves burgers, but what to do when you're on a keto diet, and you can't use any bread? The answer is to replace the buns with fried eggplant slices. You are in for a treat with this unusual dish as one single bite contains eggplant, burger, and melted cheese layers. Yummy!

Preparation Time	Servings	Calories Per Serving
1-hour total cooking time	4	585 Calories

Ingredients:

- 850g ground Beef meat
- 2 large Eggplants (male, check the bottom of eggplant for indentation, if you see a circle that's a male, a line means that's a female, you need to get 2 large male eggplants for this dish as they contain less seed)
- 3 Onions, diced thoroughly
- 2 tablespoons avocado oil
- 2 diced Jalapeno peppers (with seeds)
- Salt, variable to taste
- Black pepper, variable to taste
- 3 tablespoons cream Cheese
- 80g grated Cheddar Cheese (alternatively parmesan)

- ½ teaspoon Garlic powder
- Minced Garlic cloves, variable to how many eggplant slices you make
- 1 teaspoon of fresh Coriander leaves, chopped well
- 2 teaspoons of fresh Parsley leaves, also chopped well

Preparation

01 Let's start by preheating the oven to 180C (356°).
02 Prepare two mixing bowls.
03 Place the cream cheese, parmesan (or cheddar), diced jalapenos, garlic powder, and mix them together.
04 In the second mixing bowl, place the meat, spices, and onions. Mix very well by hand.
05 Create your burger slices and make sure you don't make them too thin.
06 Take a spoon and fill the center of the burgers with the cheese from the first bowl.
07 Make sure you engulf the cheese from all sides. It's ok if some streaks appear.
08 Once the burgers are ready, using a brush, coat them with avocado oil (or olive oil if you want).
09 Place them on aluminum foil on a broiling pan and put them into the oven's mid-section. Careful when handling preheated ovens.
10 Broil until both upper and undersides are cooking very well (check frequently).
11 Once the burgers are ready, turn off the oven and leave them inside.
12 Prepare a frying pan and set on medium heat, use avocado oil to coat it.

13 Slice the eggplants into circles, throw away the stem and the bottom.
14 Cut off the black skin layer from the circle sides.
15 Salt the eggplants, but not too much. A pinch on each slice.
16 Fry them in the pan until they are browned and done.
17 Once you have 2 slices per burger, set pan aside.
18 Put eggplant slices on a plate and add minced garlic clove 1 per each slice.
19 Make traditional burgers with eggplant slices on top and bottom.
20 Add the coriander and parsley leaves into the burger, between the meat and eggplant.
21 Serve hot.
22 Enjoy!

There is an alternative way of cooking this recipe, instead of broiling the burgers in the oven you can traditionally grill them for 10 minutes each side on medium heat. And instead of beef, you could always try turkey meat.

Grilled Flank Steak with Avocado Dip

Summertime is here, you've got your grill set up and ready, and you can't wait to show off your BBQ mastery to your friends, or maybe you're spending a quiet weekend afternoon with the family, and you decide to grill a nice juicy steak for everyone. I'm here to help you make the most of it with this outstanding dish.

 Preparation Time 15 minutes for the dip, 1-hour total cooking time	 Servings 6
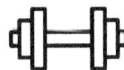 Calories per serving of Avocado dip 110 Calories	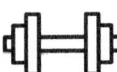 Calories per serving of Flank Stake 674 calories

Ingredients for Avocado Dip:

- 3 large Avocados, no seeds or peels
- 3.5 tablespoons Olive oil
- ¼ teaspoon Salt
- ¼ teaspoon Black pepper
- ½ teaspoon apple cider vinegar
- 80g fresh Basil
- Juice of 1 whole Lemon

- 30g pine nuts
- ¼ teaspoon dry mint, barely a hint

Ingredients for Flank steak:

- 1400g Flank Steak (beef)
- 1 cup Coconut aminos
- 1.5 tablespoon Chili pepper, powder
- 1 tablespoon Salt
- 3 teaspoons Thyme, dry
- Juice from 1.5 Lemons
- 170g Apple Cider Vinegar
- 1 cup Olive oil, extra virgin
- 5 Garlic cloves, peeled and mashed
- 1 tablespoon Onion powder
- 1 tablespoon Oregano, dry
- ½ teaspoon Rosemary
- Zest from half small Lemon

Preparation

01 First, we are going to make the dip, which should be relatively easy.
02 Using a hot pan, you need to dry roast the pine nuts until golden, be careful as they burn easily, and you should stir them frequently.
03 Once that's done, set them aside.
04 Peel and de-seed the avocados then carve out the edible part.

05 Place it in a blender along with 2 tablespoons of olive oil, then add salt, black pepper, vinegar, basil, lemon juice, a pinch of the pine nuts, and dry mint.
06 Process them until the substance is pasty smooth.
07 Place in a bowl, decorate with remaining pine nuts and olive oil and set in the fridge for when the steak is ready.
08 Make sure your steak isn't too large for the grill, cut into parts if necessary. But not too small.
09 Next, we're going to marinade the steak in a glass bowl and cover it with plastic wrap.
10 You make the marinade by poking the meat parts with a fork a few times making holes where the marinade can enter.
11 Place the meat in the glass bowl, along with the coconut aminos, the chili pepper, the salt, thyme, lemon juice, vinegar (very important), olive oil, garlic cloves, onion powder, oregano, rosemary and lemon zest.
12 Place your glass bowl in a fridge for 24 hours (the longer you marinade, the better, more tender meat) Or alternatively, you can marinade it in room temperature for about 45 minutes. Just make sure your glass bowl is sealed tight with the plastic wrap.
13 Once it's marinated, you can begin grilling the steak while occasionally brushing the meat with the marinade using a brush. (the brushing is optional).
14 Make sure both sides of the meat are cooked properly.
15 Once your steak is ready, serve with lightly grilled Brussel sprouts, baby onions and the avocado dip from the fridge.
16 Decorate with Basil leaves. Enjoy!

Every chef should have at least 1 grilled steak recipe up their sleeve. This steak is traditionally marinated in mustard, but I found that not everyone likes the punch that mustard brings and instead I opted for the Italian greens (thyme, oregano) because they go very well with beef.

Stuffed Mushrooms and Zucchini

This delicious meal is not only fun to cook, but it's an incredibly nutritious low-carb variation of the traditional stuffed vegetable style of cooking. Surely, you've tried stuffed peppers, tomatoes, and other delicacies. But have you ever really stuffed mushrooms with bacon? I didn't think so.

Preparation Time
30 minutes for stuffed mushrooms, 50 minutes for stuffed zucchinis, approx. 2-hours total cooking time.

Servings
6 servings of mushrooms, 6 servings of zucchini

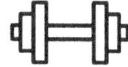

Calories per serving of stuffed Mushrooms
409 Calories

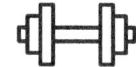

Calories per serving of stuffed Zucchini
480 Calories

Ingredients for Stuffed Mushrooms:

- 14 Mushrooms
- 280g Bacon
- 1 tablespoon Olive oil
- Salt, variable to taste
- Black pepper, variable to taste
- 40g Parmesan, home grated
- 180g Cream Cheese

- 1 teaspoon Turmeric, dry powder
- 4 tablespoons fresh chopped Chives

Ingredients for Stuffed Zucchini:

- 2 large Zucchinis
- 400g low-fat Mozzarella
- 5 teaspoons Olive oil, extra virgin
- 2 teaspoons Italian Seasoning
- 180g chopped and diced Onion, white
- 250g low-carb Marinara sauce
- 2 green peppers, chopped and diced into small cubes
- 3 teaspoons Garlic powder
- 500g ground Beef, low fat
- 450g ground Turkey, low fat
- 30g fresh Basil leaves, chopped
- Pinch of salt, variable to taste

Preparation

01 First, we are going to prepare the stuffed mushrooms.
02 You will preheat your oven to 200C (392°).
03 Using a skillet, fry the bacon well. Once it's done take it out of skillet but don't throw away the fat.
04 Let bacon cool down then mash it into little crumbs.
05 Cut the stems from the mushrooms and separate them, now dice and chop all the stems into little pieces.
06 Add the diced stems into the bacon skillet (fat) and cook them, then set aside once done. (add olive oil if it gets too dry).

07 Put the mushroom heads upside down on a baking pan.
08 Prepare a bowl for mixing, place the bacon crumbs and the stems inside, then add the salt, black pepper, parmesan, turmeric, cream cheese, and chives.
09 Mix well and using a spoon place one scoop over each mushroom filling its center.
10 Once all mushrooms are "stuffed" bake them in the oven for 15 minutes.
11 Keep an eye on this, once the mushrooms are goldened you can take them out.
12 Place aside (we will reheat this once the zucchini is finished later).
13 Keep the oven running.
14 Season the ground beef and turkey in a bowl and cover it with a plastic wrap.
15 Secondly, we will not prepare the stuffed zucchini.
16 Lower the oven heat down to 175C (347°).
17 Add olive oil to new skillet (frying pan), set to medium heat and sauté the chopped onion, green peppers, add the garlic powder and once everything is brown and juicy add the ground beef and turkey.
18 Make sure the meat was pre-seasoned earlier step 14.
19 Cook until almost dry then adds the marinara sauce.
20 Simmer for 15 minutes.
21 Set aside and let it cool down a little.
22 Add grated cheese to it and stir a little bit, so it isn't on the surface.
23 Grab your zucchinis and cut them into 2-3-inch cup-shaped slices.
24 Get rid of both ends.
25 Using a sharp knife (Careful!) or a proper zucchini corer, carve out the inside of the zucchini to make a place for the stuffing.
26 Note: You can keep the insides of zucchini in the fridge and fry them later with some eggs, different meal, well worth it.

27 Make sure the bottom layer of the cup isn't too thin or else it will leak once we cook it.
28 Prepare parchment paper on a baking pan and place the zucchinis on it.
29 Start filling your zucchinis with the enticing meat mixture you made.
30 Don't be afraid to put a little bit over the tip.
31 Place this luscious pan into the oven and bake for 15-20 minutes.
32 Pull pan out of the oven (use oven mitts).
33 Sprinkle all the remaining cheese on top of the zucchini cups, make a mess you've earned the right to!
34 Put the pan back into the oven and bake the cups.
35 Check frequently after 15-20 minutes to make sure the zucchini is tender, and the cheese is golden brown.
36 Take pan out.
37 Place mushrooms back into the oven just to reheat them.
38 Serve both together hot.
39 Enjoy!

While this meal is a little too ambitious, I promise you that once you push your fork into either one of the meals, and you take a heavenly bite you will understand the true meaning of "fruits of my labor." This meal is a perfect party dish and goes well with most salads.

WAIT! BEFORE YOU GO AHEAD!

Don't miss your free gift...

I put a lot of effort into creating it, and I'd be proud if you would take a look at it.

If you haven't received it yet, go to this URL and I'll send your "**surprise gift**" directly to your messenger.

www.cj-caldwell.com/surprise

DINNER

Most of us don't have the time nor luxury to spend evening hours in the kitchen, let's face it, by the time the sun sets we're usually in our mellow, relaxed self after a day's worth of achievements. For those of us who have families and especially children, I know that dinner must be cooked quickly, in a simple manner, and most of all the meals must be lightweight. For these reasons, I have prepared seven of the finest, healthiest, most enjoyable keto dinner recipes for you.

King Tabbouleh Salad

My first choice goes to the Middle Eastern favorite king salad, the royalty comes due to an ancient tradition that tabbouleh must always be present on the dinner table. Traditionally eaten as an appetizer or side dish in most middle eastern countries. The classic recipe contains bulgur, which is a no-no for a keto diet. However, I've found that substituting the little bulgur grains with cauliflower rice not only makes it healthier, but it tastes even better than before especially if you give the cauliflower a 3-minute fry before making the rice.

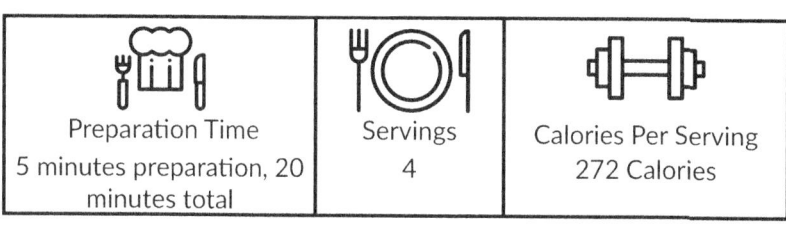

Preparation Time	Servings	Calories Per Serving
5 minutes preparation, 20 minutes total	4	272 Calories

Ingredients :

- 3/4 cauliflower head
- 350g small tomatoes, remove seeds and dice into ½ cm pieces
- 80g Shallot, peel well and dice into very small pieces like we did with tomatoes
- 200g fresh Parsley, flat-leaf specifically, chopped including tops of stems
- 50g fresh Mint Leaves
- ¼ teaspoon Cinnamon powder
- Salt, variable to taste

- Black pepper, variable to taste
- ¼ or a hint of Chili pepper. (if you like the salad slightly spicy)
- ½ teaspoon Sumac, powder
- Juice of one large Lemon
- 100ml Olive oil, extra virgin
- 4 Lettuce leaves for each serving

Preparation

01 Prepare a skillet and fry the cauliflower for about 2 minutes. You want it between raw and cooked.
02 Drain and place cauliflower in a blender, pulse until grained (don't overdo it as you don't want a pasty-puree substance, think grains of rice).
03 When done, place in large bowl and set aside, this will be your main bowl for the meal.
04 Using a serrated knife, finely dice the tomatoes into extra small pieces then put them in the cauliflower bowl. Make sure you don't add any seeds or juice.
05 Chop the mint and parsley leaves into 2-3mm with a very sharp knife, add to bowl.
06 Dice the shallots into small pieces and add to the bowl.
07 Add the olive oil, lemon juice, salt, pepper, chili, sumac, and cinnamon.
08 Mix everything very well.
09 When serving, put the desired amount into a smaller serving bowl and decorate with 4 lettuce leaves on each side.
10 You can alternatively serve the tabbouleh as a stuffing to fresh, large lettuce leaves.

11. Enjoy!

Now while this is a simple, lightweight dinner salad, don't let it fool you as it goes perfectly well with a variety of meats. Especially if the meat has been grilled. It's common to see tabbouleh served next to kebab or grilled lamb meat in the middle east. Also, it goes well with my breakfast recipe the Baba Ghanoush. Tabbouleh can store easily and stay fresh in the fridge for 24 hours. Note: make sure the vegetables are all diced into very small pieces as that's the secret technique to making a king tabbouleh.

Chicken and Spinach Supper

One of the wonders of the skillet is how quickly and easy you can prepare dinners and breakfasts. Some even in less than 15 minutes, like this wonderful chicken and spinach dish almost specifically made for a quick snack in the evening.

Preparation Time	Servings	Calories Per Serving
10-15 minutes total cooking time	4	650 Calories

Ingredients :

- 1200g Chicken breasts, skinned and washed
- 1.5 large Onion, white
- Juice from one large Lemon
- 2 tablespoons Avocado oil
- Salt, variable to taste
- Black pepper, variable to taste
- 300g baby Bella Mushrooms
- 400g frozen Spinach
- 30g fresh Basil leaves, chopped
- 1 teaspoon Garlic, powder

Preparation

01 Oil your favorite deep (emphasis on deep) skillet and put in the diced onion.
02 Slice the mushrooms and add them to the onion.
03 Cook until onion is translucent and fragrant.
04 Slice the chicken into little bites (but not too little) Add them to the pan. Cook the chicken for 6-8 minutes.
05 Add basil, salt, pepper, garlic and stir.
06 Add the spinach and set to low heat.
07 Add the lemon juice, careful not to drop any lemon seeds in.
08 If it gets dry (it shouldn't because the spinach was frozen), then add a little bit of oil.
09 Put into serving plates when chicken is cooked thoroughly.
10 Enjoy!

Best served with our keto bread mentioned before, you may also prepare this meal differently if you want, you can use a grill instead of a skillet and grill the chicken, instead of baby Bella mushrooms you can get large ones and maybe add some grilled tomatoes to the mix. You can't go wrong with a chicken and spinach combination, and best of all it's all keto friendly.

Coconut Shrimp Soup

A lot of people think that soups are most fitting for the winters. However, I found that some soups are just made for summer, especially when there's seafood involved. This exquisite Brazilian dinner is the perfect example of how tasty soups can be without spending too much time in preparation.

Preparation Time	Servings	Calories Per Serving
15-20 minutes total cooking time	6	347 Calories

Ingredients :

- 700g Shrimp, peeled and deveined (raw)
- 60g Olive oil
- Salt, variable to taste
- Black pepper, variable to taste
- Juice of two large Limes
- 240g Coconut milk
- 2 Onions, diced thoroughly
- 1 Garlic clove, minced
- 50g Red Pepper, diced
- 75g fresh Coriander (or Cilantro) leaves, chopped
- 400g diced Tomatoes, canned
- 1.5 tablespoon Sriracha hot sauce
- 1 teaspoon Oregano, powder

Preparation

01 Set a saucepan over medium heat.
02 Add the oil and sauté the onions until tender and translucent.
03 Add the pepper, garlic, tomatoes.
04 Stir and cook for a few minutes.
05 Add the shrimp and cilantro and cook until shrimp is done.
06 Pour coconut milk and sriracha sauce.
07 Cook well but don't let it boil.
08 Finally add the lime, salt, pepper, and oregano.
09 Stir for another 2 minutes and make sure shrimp is well cooked.
10 Enjoy!

With this technique you can introduce a wide range of soup variations into your dinner table, the reason being that you can replace the shrimp with chicken and it would still be as delicious. If you are adventurous enough, you can also cook white fish meat the same way. These meats work very well with this soup and will serve as a perfect dinner for you and your loved ones.

Pork Loin with Broccoli

A variation of the stir-fried Chinese pork. The broccoli and ginger provide a rich taste as the pork melts with every bite. A must-have in every weekly dinner plan.

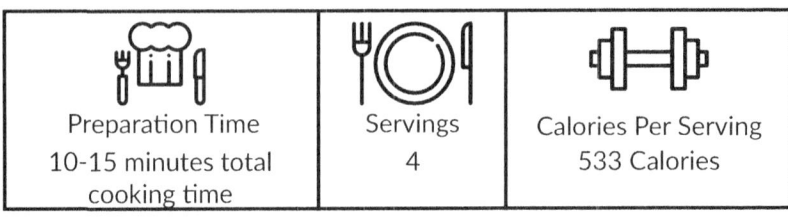

| Preparation Time 10-15 minutes total cooking time | Servings 4 | Calories Per Serving 533 Calories |

Ingredients :

- 450g Pork loin, sliced into strips
- 2 tablespoons Coconut aminos
- 1 tablespoon Ginger, fresh and minced (without skin layer)
- 4 strips Scallions, cut into 1.5-inch pieces
- ½ teaspoon crushed Red Pepper (flake)
- ½ teaspoon Poppy seeds
- 2.5 tablespoons Olive oil
- 3 small Garlic cloves, minced
- 400g Broccoli Florets
- 1 red Bell Pepper, sliced into strips
- 1 tablespoon Coconut sugar (or another keto sweetener)
- 1 teaspoon Sesame oil
- 1 teaspoon Rosemary
- ½ tablespoon Tamari soy sauce
- ¼ tablespoon cornstarch (increasing the amount will exceed the carb limits of a keto diet)

Preparation

01 Prepare 3 mixing bowls and one deep enough pan (or wok if you can).
02 Combine the minced garlic, ginger, pork loin strips and 1 tablespoon of olive oil in the first bowl.
03 Add the rosemary and mix well.
04 In the second bowl, you will put the red bell pepper strips, the scallions, and broccoli florets (bite-sized).
05 In the third bowl, you will make the stir fry sauce, add the sweetener, tamari sauce, sesame oil, poppy seeds, red pepper flakes, coconut aminos, and cornstarch (emphasis on the very little amount of cornstarch, ¼ of a tablespoon just to thicken the sauce slightly).
06 Set your pan on high heat and give it a thin coating of olive oil.
07 Add the contents of the pork loins bowl to the pan and cook until the meat has almost finished cooking.
08 Remove the pork from the pan and put back into its bowl.
09 Stir fry the vegetables from the second bowl in the same pan.
10 Keep stirring and flipping the vegetables as we don't want them to be fully cooked just yet.
11 Once they are tender and halfway done, put the pork back in the pan and add the sauce bowl as well.
12 Stir for 10 minutes on high heat and make sure everything is cooked, especially the pork.
13 Serve in bowls, sprinkle more poppy seeds and the slightest hint of salt on top.
14 Enjoy!

Alternatively, you may want to exclude the cornstarch entirely and instead just use a scoop of butter instead. But you'd have to be careful about your daily intake. Or, if you'd like you can remove the contents of the bowl and leave the sauce to boil until desired thickness then pour it on top of the already cooked pork and vegetables. This broccoli may also be replaced by avocadoes in case you're wondering what other delicious combinations you can try.

Turkey Bacon and Chicken Meatballs

It sounds elaborate and strange, but this dish is far easier than you imagined and while your dish will look like an Easter basket, it will soon become a hit on your weekly to-cook list.

Preparation Time	Servings	Calories Per Serving
15 minutes total cooking time	3	543 Calories (135,7 per ball)

Ingredients :

- 600g ground Chicken meat
- 20 slices of Turkey Bacon
- ½ teaspoon Garlic powder
- 1.5 teaspoon Onion powder
- Salt, variable to taste
- Black pepper, variable to taste
- 1.5 tablespoon paprika
- 1 tablespoon Olive Oil
- ½ teaspoon Basil, dry

Preparation

01 Prepare a mixing bowl.
02 Add the turkey bacon into the bowl, pour the onion and garlic powders, then add the salt, black pepper, dry basil, and paprika and mix very well.
03 Rub a few drops of olive oil on your hands and grab some meat, then roll it into balls (it takes some practice if this is your first time).
04 Make 10 meatballs with this quantity of meat.
05 For each meatball, grab two slices of bacon and wrap it around them.
06 You are now a master of bacon wraps.
07 Set a skillet over medium heat and pour in the olive oil, but not too much.
08 Start adding 3 meatballs at a time and cook them until they are noticeably well cooked.
09 Set to low heat and continue for 5 minutes.
10 You want the bacon to be hard, but not crispy or burnt.
11 Enjoy!

Best served with avocado dip. However, bacon goes well with almost anything, so you could just as easily hard boil a few eggs and make a proper Easter basket, or you could substitute the turkey with normal bacon instead of turkey. Get creative with this fun, light recipe.

Spicy Mushroom Soup

In Hungary, it would be considered strange if there wasn't at least 1 spicy soup served during the week. This delicious soup will surely test your taste buds and strength as we're going all out on the spices and I promise you'll love every bit of it. Note: you will need to make or buy chick stock for this one.

Preparation Time	Servings	Calories Per Serving
1-hour total cooking time	6	342 Calories

Ingredients for Chicken stock:

- 400g Chicken bones
- Bunch of bay leaves
- 1 Cinnamon stick
- 4 peeled Garlic cloves
- 1 whole white Onion (chopped in half)

Ingredients for mushroom soup:

- 500g fresh Mushrooms
- 3.5 tablespoons Butter
- 100g Sour Cream
- 350g chopped Onions, white

- 400g chicken Stock
- 1.5 tablespoon Paprika
- ½ tablespoon Soy sauce
- Half a large Lemon Juice
- 1.5 teaspoon Dili, dry
- 220g heavy whipping cream
- Black pepper, variable to taste
- 2 jalapenos sliced
- 1.5 teaspoon Salt
- 1 teaspoon hot Chili powder
- Bunch of fresh, chopped Parsley leaves
- ¼ teaspoon Mint, dry

Preparation

01 Refer to the "Cauliflower and chicken thigh bowl" recipe and make the same chicken stock.
02 Prepare a large soup pot and set to medium heat.
03 Add the butter and melt it.
04 Add the mushrooms and sauté for 3-5 minutes.
05 Add the onions and sauté for 3 minutes, until translucent.
06 Pour in the chicken stock.
07 Add the sliced jalapenos.
08 Stir while adding the soy sauce and Dili.
09 Cover, and let it simmer on low heat for about 10 minutes.
10 Pour heavy whipping cream and stir continuously for 2 minutes.
11 Stop stirring and cover.
12 Cook for 10 minutes and then add salt, pepper, hot chili powder, sour cream, mint and lemon juice.

13 Let it cook for another 5 minutes.
14 Serve and Enjoy!

You can decorate the bowls with the parsley leaves and sprinkle a little bit of dry mint on top. This soup goes very well with our keto bread recipe, and in case you feel that the spices are to be avoided then just don't add the jalapenos or hot chili powder and you're set.

Coconut Skirt Steak with Swiss Chard

Skirt steak is a plate beef meat that is usually mistaken for flank due to the location of the cut. However this meat is not very tender as much as it's flavorful, and for this recipe, we will complement it with cauliflower rice as it goes very well with it.

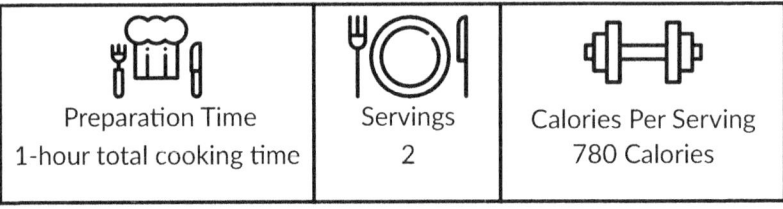

Preparation Time 1-hour total cooking time	Servings 2	Calories Per Serving 780 Calories

Ingredients:

- 180g Coconut oil
- 900g Skirt steak
- 4 Garlic cloves, minced
- 1.5 teaspoon red Pepper flakes
- Juice of two Limes
- Zest of one Lime
- 60g pine nuts
- 1 teaspoon Salt
- 1.5 teaspoon Turmeric, dry
- 450g chopped Swiss chard
- 200g Cauliflower heads
- 1 tablespoon Olive Oil

Preparation

01 Cut the leaves and base of the cauliflower root.
02 Chop cauliflower into chunks.
03 Heat a skillet over medium heat, dry roast the pine nuts just until they are golden (but don't brown them).
04 Remove the pine nuts from pan and into a dish for garnishing later.
05 Put your cauliflower into a blender or food processor and pulse them until they are almost the same shape as rice.
06 Don't pulse it too long or it will become pasty.
07 Spread the cauliflower in a baking pan, sprinkle some olive oil on top of them.
08 Roast the cauliflower rice for about 10 minutes at 180C (356°).
09 Take the cauliflower out of the oven and set aside for later.
10 Prepare a large mixing bowl.
11 Add the coconut oil (melted), zest and juice from the limes, red pepper flakes, turmeric, and salt and mix well.
12 Cut the skirt steak into two pieces.
13 Place both into the bowl and cover it with plastic wrap.
14 Wash the swiss chard.
15 Let it marinade for half an hour at room temperature.
16 Place a large enough skillet to medium heat and pour everything in the marinade bowl in it once the skillet is hot.
17 Put the Swiss chard into the skillet.
18 Cook and seer the skirt steak until it's ready.
19 Put it on the serving plate and compliment with cauliflower rice.
20 Sprinkle the golden pine nuts on top.
21 Enjoy!

It might be a little heavy for dinner, but how can you resist those roasted pine nuts on top of that hearty steak? Alternatively, you can replace the cauliflower rice with spinach or kale, and it would still be just as amazing.

Feedback

I'm glad you have read all the way to this point. Hopefully, you liked the recipes; I hope that they could encourage you to cook often and live a healthy life.

It took me months of work to finish this book. I have invested my time, effort, passion and nerves to offer you the best possible recipes. I have cooked every single recipe countless times.

I would be honored to receive any feedback from you about the recipes and even photos if you have cooked some of them.

When you visit the URL below, you can connect to me in your messenger, and we can directly chat with each other.

www.cj-caldwell.com/feedback

Please don't hold back from writing me if you …

- Want to give me feedback.
- Have cooked the recipes.
- Found any mistakes that I should know about.
- Have any suggestions for improvements.
- Have anything else.

I appreciate every opinion and feedback. I would love to improve my recipes, this cookbook and my passion for writing. Books are nothing without their readers.

Images & Layout

Book Layout by
Shahid Jewel | Designscozy | shahidseu09@gmail.com

Graphics used:

© Fotolia
File: #132146950 | by: great_kit
File: #136190619 | by: makalo86
File: #184688309 | by: vectorgoods
File: #110989588 | by: kate_sun
File: #88706061 | by: Natalya Levish
File: #46809980 | by: oleksajewicz
File: #168850870 | by: oksanaok

Printed in Great Britain
by Amazon